LANCASHIRE TRACTION

Ross Taylor

AMBERLEY

First published 2015

Amberley Publishing
The Hill, Stroud
Gloucestershire, GL5 4EP

www.amberley-books.com

Copyright © Ross Taylor, 2015

The right of Ross Taylor to be identified as
the Author of this work has been asserted in
accordance with the Copyrights, Designs and
Patents Act 1988.

ISBN 978 1 4456 4316 8 (print)
ISBN 978 1 4456 4332 8 (ebook)

British Library Cataloguing in Publication Data.
A catalogue record for this book is available from
the British Library.

Typesetting by Amberley Publishing.
Printed in the UK.

Introduction

My intention for this publication is to promote the different and varied traction within Lancashire, and to cover its brief history. The four main lines that are covered in Lancashire are as follows: the West Coast Main Line, which runs from Coppull to Carnforth, passing through the main station hub for Lancashire (Preston), the old market town of Garstang and Catterall. The journey on this line then heads into the university city of Lancaster, then on to its final leg passing the coast at Hest Bank before reaching Carnforth. The second line covered here is the Ribble Valley line, which runs from Blackburn to Hellifield and passes through the scenic countryside of the Ribble Valley. After departing Blackburn the line cuts off at Daisyfield Junction and heads down the 10-mile section to Clitheroe, passing through Ramsgreave and Wilpshire, Langho and the iconic forty-eight-arched Whalley Viaduct, built between 1846 and 1850 and consisting of over 7 million bricks and over 12,338 cubic metres of stone. The viaduct has to be one of the most picturesque viaducts not just on this line but in the whole of the UK. After crossing over the viaduct the line weaves its way past Clitheroe golf club and into the market town itself. Clitheroe has won one of thirty-six Outstanding Natural Beauty awards and has the smallest Norman castle in the whole of the UK; it was built in 1186 by Robert de Lacy. After leaving Clitheroe the line twists and turns, heading through Chatburn, and continues into the countryside as it climbs through Rimington and into Gisburn. After heading through Gisburn, the line curves round through Gisburn tunnel and climbs into Newsholme; this is where the border for North Yorkshire starts and the line carries on a couple of miles to Hellifield. Onto the third line, heading towards the Fylde Coast of Blackpool passing through Salwick, Kirkham and Wesham, Poulton-le-Fylde, Leyton and into its final destination of Blackpool North. The fourth and final main route is the Copy Pit line, also known as the Calverdale Line, which runs direct over the West Pennine Moors from Preston to Leeds. The line has to challenge the 1 in 68 incline from Stansfield Hall to Copy Pit Summit near a small hamlet called Portsmouth, where the line crosses the border into South Yorkshire.

Lancashire sees a wide variety of freight companies, such as DB Schenker, Freightliner, Colas Rail and Direct Rail Services. Also, it has a variety of locomotives to choose from, such as the new Class 68 or the old Class 37, not to forget Class 33s from the West Coast Railway Company at Carnforth. With Direct Rail Services getting stronger, they have managed to get the majority of Lancashire work such as nuclear flasks, container services, and departmental movements. The photographs brought together in this publication have all been taken by the author and cover the last decade of Lancashire traction.

Many more pictures are available on my Flickr account: www.flickr.com/photos/54630706@N02/.

Ross Taylor, Clitheroe
September 2014

In the summer the back lines between Lostock Hall and Hellifield see a variety of different steam excursions such as the 'Cumbrian Mountain Express' and 'The Fellsman'. Here we see LMS Princess Coronation Class 46233 *Duchess of Sutherland* passing Clitheroe with the 1Z21 'Cumbrian Mountain Express', which runs from Crewe to Carlisle. This train runs all year round and sees all seasons. It is seen here on Saturday 30 August 2014.

After entering service in November 1957, Class 31 31105 sits at Preston with the 1Q05 Longsight Car MD–Springs Branch Jn at Wigan with a Network Rail test train via Ormskirk and Hebden Bridge, on the evening of Thursday 4 September 2014.

Standing in for DB Schenker are two of DRS's finest English Electric Type 3s, 37603 and 37402, seen here passing Newsholme with the Pathfinder Tours return working of the 1Z83 'The Pennine Explorer', which ran from Carlisle to Taunton on Wednesday 9 July 2014.

Direct Rail Services English Electric Type 3s are seen passing Clitheroe with the 2Q08 10.00 Mossend–Derby RTC Network Rail test train, on Saturday 2 May 2009.

Compass Tours 1Z76 'The Mersey Fellsman' is seen passing Rimington with Brush Type 4 47802 at the helm. This tour originated at Liverpool and was travelling to Carlisle. On the rear of the train was 47712, which sadly got removed at Carlisle due to a fault with the traction motors. It is seen here on Saturday 12 June 2010.

Fragonset Class 47 47703 arrives at Clitheroe train station with the 1Z54 'The Edinburgh Fellsman', which ran from Layton near Blackpool to Edinburgh Waverley. The now preserved Brush Class 47 sadly no longer runs on the main line. It is seen here on Saturday 23 September 2006.

No. 66414 *James the Engine* speeds past Hest Bank with the 4M16 Grangemouth–Daventry container service, seen here on the evening of Saturday 22 May 2010. The GM Class 66 sadly left DRS and is now owned by Freightliner. The Class 66 was painted into Stobart colours, along with 66411 *Eddie the Engine*, for the contract of the 4S43 Tesco train.

Heaton (Newcastle)-based 142089 departs Clitheroe with the 2J50 12.44 Clitheroe–Manchester Victoria service, seen here on Thursday 18 July 2013. Class 142s were banned from using the line between Blackburn and Hellifield until 16 August 2012. The first of its class was 142005, which came into Clitheroe with the 16.24 Manchester Victoria–Clitheroe service and departed with the 18.06 Clitheroe–Manchester Victoria service.

West Coast Railways Crompton's Class 33s 33029 and 33207 pass Wennington with the return working of the 1Z23 Lancaster–Cleethorpes, seen here on the rear of the train. No. 57601 was on the front of the train.

Direct Rail Services' 57007, 57003 and 37607 are seen passing Clitheroe on Friday 14 March 2014 with the 0K05 Carlisle Kingmoor Sidings–Crewe Basford Hall light engine move. This train normally runs as the 6K05 from Carlisle yard but due to Network Rail having no traffic, DRS used it for them to do a locomotive move.

Network Rail has been improving its lines around the Settle Junction area. Freightliner Class 66 66620 passes Whalley with the 6Y07 Settle Junction–Crewe Basford Hall ballast drop move, seen here on Saturday 24 March 2007.

Colas Rail Class 66 66849 *Wylam Dilly* is seen climbing over the brow at Newsholme with the 6J37 Carlisle Yard Colas Rail–Chirk Kronospan loaded log train. This service runs from Monday to Saturday and can travel via either the Settle & Carlisle or the WCML. It was seen here on Thursday 6 September 2012.

DRS choppers 20303 and 20304 thrash past Houghton with Spitfire's rail tour 1Z20, Birmingham International–Carlisle via the famous Settle & Carlisle, seen here on Saturday 7 February 2009. On the rear of the train was West Coast Rail Company Class 57 57601.

EWS-liveried Class 66 66117, now owned by DB Schenker, is seen as it is departing Clitheroe with the 6Z74 Clitheroe Castle Cement–Leicester loaded cement train, seen here on Saturday 22 May 2010. This train ran to help build the London Olympic stadium at Stratford.

Freightliner Class 66 66618 powers past Woodacre on the West Coast Main Line with the 6Y58 Oubeck–Crewe Basford Hall engineering train, seen here on Sunday 1 April 2007.

After the failure of 67006 at Doncaster, EWS-liveried 67008 stepped in to work the remaining portion of the 13.02 1Z25 London King's Cross–Burnley Manchester Road football special. The train is seen arriving into Blackburn Up and Down goods loop, ready to run around and work back to London, on Monday 18 August 2014.

DB Schenker super tug 60024 is seen passing Portsmouth, nearly crossing the border into West Yorkshire, with the return working 6E32 Preston Docks–Lindsey Oil Refinery empty bitumen tanks, on Wednesday 2 July 2014.

Colas Rail's Class 66 66848 climbs up the gradient at Ramsgreave and Wilpshire with the 6J37 Carlisle Yard Colas Rail–Chirk Kronospan, on Tuesday 19 June 2012.

No. 66122 arrives into Clitheroe with the 6M94 Avonmouth Hansons Siding–Clitheroe Castle Cement empty tanks, seen here on Tuesday 19 August 2014. This train runs three days a week: on Tuesday, Thursday and Saturday.

DB Schenker super tug 60024 sits at Clitheroe Castle Cement as part of the 2014 open day. The Class 60 worked in from Doncaster Belmont yard the night before and was the main feature at the open day; the Class 60 held the nameplate *Clitheroe Castle*, which was originally on 60029. It is seen here on Saturday 20 September 2014.

After being built by Armstrong Whitworth in 1936, LMS Stanier Class 5 4-6-0 45231 *Sherwood Forester* is seen passing Clitheroe with Statesman Rails 1Z52 'The Fellsman', which runs from Lancaster to Carlisle on summer Wednesdays and is seen here on Wednesday 20 August 2014.

Ex Arriva Trains Wales-liveried 57313 is seen now working for West Coast Railways as it approaches Whalley train station after crossing the forty-eight-arched Whalley Viaduct. The Class 57 was standing in for 60009 *Union of South Africa*, which couldn't work the train due to Network Rail having a steam ban. The working was the 1Z21, the Rail Touring Company's 'Cumbrian Mountain Express', seen here on Saturday 16 August 2014.

After arriving in the country in early 2014 from General Electric in Pennsylvania, 70802 makes light work of the 6J37 Carlisle Yard Colas Rail–Chirk Kronospan as it passes Clitheroe. The Class 70 was removed at Warrington Bank Quay; the Class 56, 56105, seen behind the Class 70 would take the train forward to Chirk. This photograph was taken on Saturday 26 July 2014.

After being built between 1846 and 1850, the forty-eight-arched Whalley Viaduct is still standing strong and is a listed structure. No. 66520 slowly passes over the viaduct with the 6M11 Hunterston–Fiddlers Ferry power station loaded coal train, seen here on Wednesday 13 August 2014. The River Calder passes underneath the train, next to Whalley Abbey.

Ian Riley's Class 37 37518 arrives into Clitheroe with Statesman Rail's 1Z52, 'The Fellsman', which runs from Lancaster to Carlisle via Preston, Blackburn and Hellifield, on Wednesday 13 August 2014. The Class 37 was covering for a steam locomotive due to Network Rail having placed a steam ban because of lineside fire risks.

Freightliner Heavy Haul Class 66 66548 passes Clitheroe in a brief spell of sunshine with the 6M11 Hunterston–Fiddlers Ferry power station loaded coal train, on Tuesday 22 July 2014.

No. 66598 powers past Hest Bank in the strong summer sun with the 6Z16 Carlisle Yard–Crewe Basford Hall, running mega early, on Thursday 10 July 2014.

Network Rail's PED 31233 thrashes north past the coast at Hest Bank, near Morecambe, while in charge of the 3Z83 Derby RTC–Carlisle High Wapping Sidings test train move, in the late afternoon on Thursday 10 July 2014.

LMS Stanier Class 8F 48151 climbs up the 1 in 80 incline at Langho with the return working of 'The Fellsman', seen here on Wednesday 9 July 2014.

On 9 July 2014 Direct Rail Services ran a test run for the new flask wagons. No. 57010, top and tailed with 57002, passes Brock on the West Coast Main Line near Preston with the 6Z28 Carlisle Kingmoor Sidings DRS–Derby RTC.

Network Rail's DBSO 9701 is seen passing Gisburn with the 1Q14 09.14 Carlisle High Wapping Sidings–Blackburn test train. Direct Rail Services' Class 37 37601 is on the rear.

Network Rail's PED, also known as a Goyle, 31465 passes Brownhill near Blackburn with the 1Q05 Neville Hill–Derby RTC, seen here on Friday 1 August 2014. No. 97301 was on the rear of the train.

LMS Stanier Class 8F 48151 passes Rimington with the 1Z52 Lancaster–Carlisle, 'The Fellsman'. Due to Network Rail having a steam ban, the steam engine was being pushed by Ian Riley's 37518 on the rear. This photograph was taken on Wednesday 23 July 2014.

West Coast Railway Company Class 37 37516 *Loch Laidon* passes Langho with the return 1Z53 Carlisle–Lancaster, 'The Fellsman', seen here on 16 July 2014. The Class 37 replaced 8F 48151 at Carlisle due to Network Rail enforcing a steam ban because of lineside fire risks.

The first Colas Rail Class 70 to work the log train was 70802, seen here passing Hest Bank with the 6J37 Carlisle Yard Colas Rail–Chirk Kronospan loaded logs on Thursday 10 July 2014. No. 66847 was tucked in behind the Class 70.

DB Schenker Class 92 92029 *Dante* passes Carnforth with the 4Z48 Mossend–Daventry Tesco train. The Class 92 was seen here running almost thirteen hours late due to Virgin Trains Pendolino 390123 pulling the wires down in the Carlisle area the night before. It is seen here on Thursday 10 July 2014.

Colas Rail Class 66 66847 passes Preston with the 6J37 Carlisle Yard Colas Rail–Chirk Kronospan loaded log train via the West Coast Main Line, on Monday 7 July 2014.

EWS Class 66 66085 passes rival Class 66 66426 of DRS at Preston with the 0C76 Warrington Arpley–Carlisle Yard light engine move. Due to its late running, 66426 was made to stop with the 4S44 Daventry–Coatbridge FLT container train. They are seen here on Monday 7 July 2014.

Following the failure of DRS Duff 47810 during the Tour de France shuttles, the loco was dumped at Blackburn overnight. Here we have pictured DRS Northern Belle-liveried 47790 *Galloway Princess* dragging the failed Class 47 back to Crewe Gresty Bridge to receive attention. They are seen on Monday 7 July 2014.

No. 47790 leads failed 47810, which was left at Blackburn due to suffering traction motor problems, and is seen here on Monday 7 July 2014.

No. 47810 sits at Blackburn after failing on the Tour de France shuttles, which ran on Sunday 6 July 2014; the shuttles ran from Blackburn to Bradford Interchange on behalf of Northern Rail. It is seen here on the evening of Sunday 6 July 2014.

East Lancashire Railway held their diesel gala over the weekend of 5/6 July. Here we see 37324 arriving into Irwell Vale with the 11.46 2J70 Rawtenstall–Heywood service on Saturday 5 July 2014.

DB Schenker Class 60 60024 passes Lostock Hall Junction with the 6E32 Preston Docks–Lindsey oil refinery empty bitumen tanks, seen here on Wednesday 2 July 2014.

LMS Jubilee 45699 *Galatea* passes Lostock Hall with Statesman Rail's 1Z52 'The Fellsman', which runs from Lancaster to Carlisle every Wednesday in the summer. It is seen here on Wednesday 2 July 2014.

Nos 86638 and 86604 power past Hest Bank with the 4M74 Coatbridge–Crewe Basford Hall FLT container train, seen here on Tuesday 1 July 2014.

Direct Rail Services' Class 37 37611, top and tailed with 37606, passes Oxcliffe Road Bridge near Heysham with the 6C51 Sellafield–Heysham nuclear power station flask train, seen here on Tuesday 1 July 2014.

Colas Rail Class 66 66847 trundles down through Clitheroe with the 6J37 Carlisle Yard Colas Rail–Chirk loaded log train, seen here on Saturday 21 June 2014.

Freightliner Heavy Haul Class 66560 sits at Garstang and Catteral with the 6L50 from Carlisle, and is seen here in the Network Rail possession zone while waiting to collect rail in summer 2006.

Now in Direct Rail Services livery, 57304 *Pride of Cheshire* departs Preston with 0C99 Preston–Carlisle Virgin route refresher via the Settle & Carlisle. This runs in readiness for the diversions when the West Coast Main Line shuts. It is seen here on Tuesday 17 June 2014.

Colas Rail's Class 66 66847 passes Taylors House at Clitheroe with the 6J37 Carlisle Yard Colas Rail–Chirk loaded log train, on Friday 13 June 2014.

Heading away from the camera, Direct Rail Services 37606, top and tailed with 37402, passes Oxcliffe Road Bridge near Heysham with the 6C51 Sellafield–Heysham nuclear power station flask train, on Tuesday 10 June 2014.

EWS Class 66 66031 slowly passes Rishton station with the 6E32 Preston Docks–Lindsey oil refinery empty bitumen tanks. These new-looking tanks replaced the old ones in November 2010 and were put together by Axiom Rail in Stoke-on-Trent. They are seen here on Monday 9 June 2014.

Ex Virgin-liveried 57304 passes Taylors House at Clitheroe with the oC99 Preston–Carlisle Virgin route refresher, on Monday 16 June 2014.

DR 73910 passes Taylors House at Clitheroe with the 6J72 Guide Bridge Sidings–Hellifield goods loop tamper move, on Thursday 5 June 2014.

Statesman Rail's 1Z69 Carlisle–Hereford return charter special is seen passing Taylors House at Clitheroe with ex Arriva Trains Wales Class 57 57316, top and tailed with 57313, both of which are now owned by the West Coast Railway Company at Carnforth. They are seen here on Saturday 31 May 2014.

Direct Rail Services driver Ian Tunstall opens up choppers 20308 and 20309 with the 1Z21 Clitheroe Cement Works Reception Sidings–Kirkby and is pictured here passing Taylors House at Clitheroe on Saturday 31 May 2014. No. 37419 was on the rear of the train.

Direct Rail Services driver Ian Tunstall passes Rishton with the inward-bound 1Z20 Crewe–Clitheroe Castle Cement rail tour, seen here on Saturday 31 May 2014.

Colas Rail's 'Grid' 56087 passes Hest Bank near Morecambe with the 6J37 Carlisle Yard–Chirk loaded log (timber) train, seen here on Wednesday 21 May 2014.

Direct Rail Services 'Duffs' 47805 and 47853 pass Taylors House at Clitheroe with the 1Z72 Carlisle–Swindon rail tour. Thanks go to DRS driver Ian Tunstall for the thrash, seen here on Saturday 17 May 2014. In the background we can see Clitheroe Castle, which is thought to have been built back in 1186 by Robert de Lacy.

Built by Armstrong Whitworth in 1937, LMS Stanier Class 5 4-6-0 45407 *The Lancashire Fusilier*, topped and tailed with 44871, sits at Preston with the 5Z45 Cadder Yard–Castleton ELR, seen here with support coaches 35508 and 35517 on Friday 2 March 2014.

Freightliner Class 66 66513 powers through Platform 5 at Preston with the 4S42 Fiddlers Ferry–Hunterston empty HHA coal, on Thursday 1 May 2014.

Newly painted DB Schenker-liveried 66114 pulls into Clitheroe Castle Cement reception sidings with the 6S00 Clitheroe Castle Cement–Mossend loaded cement train. Here the train will run around and reverse the loaded cement onto the main line ready to head north. It is seen here on Wednesday 30 April 2014.

The weekday-running 6K05 is seen passing Horrocksford Junction at Clitheroe with 66304 in charge; the train runs from Carlisle Yard to Crewe Basford Hall and is seen here on Wednesday 30 April 2014.

Colas Rail's triple header is led by 56087, with 47739 and 56078 dead in tow as they thrash up Langho Bank with the 6V37 Ribblehead–Chirk loaded log train, seen here running three days late due to a points failure at Ribblehead on Monday 28 April 2014.

Nos 57004 and 57009 thrash past Brownhill after just climbing Langho bank with the 6K05 Carlisle Yard–Crewe Basford Hall departmental train, seen here on Monday 28 April 2014.

No. 66145 passes Brownhill with the 6Z76 Newbiggin–Arpley empty gypsum. This train runs one day a week, on Monday, Tuesday or Wednesday depending on the traffic, and is seen here on Monday 28 April 2014.

No. 66621 passes Rishton with the 4S42 Hunslet Yard–Hunterston empty coal, seen here after not running in over six months. This train runs Mondays only and is routed via the Copy Pit. It is seen here on Monday 28 April 2014.

DRS Class 66 66305 passes Blackburn with the lightly loaded 6K05 Carlisle Yard–Crewe Basford Hall departmental service, seen here on Thursday 24 April 2014.

No. 60015 passes Rishton station with the 6E32 Preston Docks–Lindsey empty bitumen tanks, on Wednesday 23 April 2014.

Colas Rail's 'Grid' 56094 passes Leyland with the Thursday-only 6S96 Sinfin–Grangemouth empty TEA tanks, seen here on Thursday 17 April 2014.

No. 60054 pulls into Preston with the returning 1Z15 Blackpool North–London Euston 'Lancashire Coast and Hills' rail tour on Thursday 17 April 2014. Here 92019 will take over the rest of the journey to London.

Freightliner Class 70 70005 sits at Preston awaiting a path with the 6Z16 Carlisle Yard–Crewe Basford Hall departmental service, on Thursday 17 April 2014.

Seeing a Class 92 parked in the bay platforms at Preston is very rare, however on Thursday 17 April 2014 92019 *Wagner* waits to depart, ready to work the onward 1Z15 to London Euston. The tour originated at Blackpool and was hauled to Preston by 60054.

Heading the 1Z12 'Lancashire Coast and Hills' rail tour from London Euston to Blackpool North is 60054, photographed passing Kirkham and Wesham on Thursday 17 April 2014.

DB Schenker have the responsibility of hauling the Royal Train, seen here with 67026 *Diamond Jubilee*, departing Blackburn after dropping off the queen, who was visiting the cathedral. On the rear was 67005, which is painted in the colour of the stock, seen here on Thursday 17 April 2014.

DB Schenker's super tug 60007 passes Rishton with the 6E32 Preston Dock–Lindsey empty bitumen tanks, seen here on Monday 14 April 2014.

DB Schenker's 126-ton Class 66 66101 passes Taylors House at Clitheroe with the 6Z35 Clitheroe Castle Cement–Bescot, on Thursday 10 April 2014.

Direct Rail Services Class 57 57004 passes Clitheroe with a very bizarre 6K05 Carlisle Kingmoor Sidings–Crewe Basford Hall departmental service, on Thursday 10 April 2014.

Direct Rail Services driver Ian Tunstall waits to cross over at Horrocksford Junction with the inward-bound 1Z20 'The Topper Chopper' rail tour, which ran from Crewe to Clitheroe Castle Cement, on Saturday 31 May 2014.

DB Schenker Class 66 66101 arrives into Clitheroe with the 6M94 Avonmouth Hansons Siding–Clitheroe Castle Cement empty tanks, on Thursday 10 April 2014.

No. 66060 passes Taylors House at Clitheroe with the 6Z76 Newbiggin–Arpley empty gypsum train, on Monday 7 April 2014.

DRS bodysnatchers 57007 and 57012 pass Clitheroe with the weekday-running 6K05 Carlisle Yard–Crewe Basford Hall departmental train, on Wednesday 19 March 2014.

LNER Class A4 4464 *Bittern* passes Newsholme with the 1Z46 Carlisle–Tyseley rail tour as far as Crewe on Saturday 15 March 2014; at Crewe 47773 will take over the remaining leg of the journey.

This service usually runs as the 6K05, but due to no traffic DRS used the path as a engine move. The 0K05 Carlisle Kingmoor DRS–Crew Basford Hall light engine is seen here on Friday 14 March 2014 passing Clitheroe station, the convoy being led by 57003, followed by 57007 and 37607 on the rear.

Nos 57007 and 57003 pass Clitheroe with the 6K05 Carlisle Yard–Crewe Basford Hall departmental service, on Tuesday 11 March 2014.

Ex Freightliner Class 57s now owned by DRS, 57003 and 57007, pass Taylors House at Clitheroe with the 6K05 Carlisle Yard–Crewe Basford Hall departmental service, on Monday 10 March 2014.

A very rare occurrence was witnessed when 37606 and 37602 worked the 6K05 Carlisle Yard–Crewe Basford Hall departmental service on Thursday 6 March 2014, and it is seen here climbing up the 1 in 80 incline at Langho.

The first ever DRS Class 37s to work the 6K05 since winning the contract of EWS/DBS back in 2013, here we see 37405, 423, 610 pass Taylors House at Clitheroe with the 6K05 Carlisle Yard–Crewe Basford Hall departmental train on Friday 28 February 2014.

Sat in the Up and Down goods loop at Preston, 66303 is seen working the 4S45 Daventry–Mossend container train on the evening of Friday 14 February 2014.

No. 56096, with 56105, storms past Brownhill with the 6J37 Carlisle Yard Colas Rail–Chirk Kronospan loaded log train, on Friday 12 September 2014. No. 56096 was on its first appearance for Colas Rail on the log train.

On hire to GBRF, but now owned by DRS, 57306 is seen as it passes Leyland with the 6G31 Oubeck Goods Loop–Crewe Basford Hall engineering train on Sunday 9 February 2014.

DB Schenker's super tugs have proved to be a success; here we see 60015 passing Taylors House at Clitheroe with the 6L48 Farrington Curve Junction–Carlisle Yard, photographed on a very dull Sunday 12 January 2014.

EWS 66139 gets a tow as sister 66132 leads the 6L52 Blackpool North–Carlisle yard engineering train north through Clitheroe, on Sunday 12 January 2014.

Autumn sees Network Rail use the water cannons to help clear the lines and prevent disruption due to leaf fall. Here we see 47818, top and tailed with 66301, standing at Preston with the 3J11 Carlisle–Carlisle via Clitheroe, Barrow-in-Furness and Windermere, awaiting departure on Wednesday 27 November 2013.

After just coming out of store DB Schenker sent Class 60 60065 to Warrington to work the 1Z67 'The Natterjack', which ran from London Euston to Southport via Manchester Victoria and the Copy Pit, seen here passing Brindle with the tour on Thursday 18 September 2014.

DRS Thunderbird 57309 *Pride of Crewe* passes Taylors House at Clitheroe with the 0P99 return Carlisle–Preston route learner for Virgin, on Thursday 17 October 2013.

Colas Rail Class 56 56087 powers past Langho station with the 6J37 Carlisle Yard Colas Rail–Chirk Kronospan loaded logs, on Saturday 12 October 2013.

Colas Rail work the 6J37 log train, which is routed via both the Settle & Carlisle and the West Coast Main Line, here 56087 powers past Broughton on the WCML with the 6J37 Carlisle Yard Colas Rail–Chirk Kronospan loaded logs, on Thursday 10 October 2013.

Due to engineering work on the Settle & Carlisle, the 6K05 was routed via the WCML and is seen here at Broughton with 66434 in charge. The train works from Carlisle Yard to Crewe Basford Hall and was photographed on Thursday 10 October 2013.

Western Champion D1015 and 47773 passes Langho with the 1Z52 Tyseley–Carlisle charter, seen here on Saturday 21 September 2013.

After recently being overhauled into the new DB Schenker super tug scheme, 60040 is seen as it passes Rishton with the 6E32 Preston Docks–Lindsey empty bitumen tanks on Wednesday 11 September 2013.

No. 66303 passes Taylors Bridge at Clitheroe in a lucky burst of afternoon sun while working the 6K05 Carlisle Yard–Crewe Basford Hall departmental on Monday 9 September 2013.

DRS 'Duffs' 47501 and 47805 pass Carnforth with the 1Z50 Carlisle–Hooton rail tour, which was routed via the Cumbrian Coast and is seen here on Wednesday 11 September 2013.

No. 66554 crawls past Carnforth station with the 6Z16 Carlisle Yard–Crewe Basford Hall departmental train as it approaches its booked stop at Carnforth goods loop, on Wednesday 11 September 2013.

Supporting Malcolm Logistics is 66434, seen passing a very wet Leyland while working the 6K05 Carlisle Yard–Crewe Basford Hall engineering train on Wednesday 11 September 2013.

Direct Rail Services have five Class 66/3s, which are all fitted with low-emission engines. Here we see 66303 passing Barrow Foot Crossing near Whalley with the 6K05 Carlisle Yard–Crewe Basford Hall engineering train, on Monday 9 September 2013.

After just crossing Whalley Viaduct, 66506 starts to climb the 1 in 80 incline up Langho bank as it curves round into a small village called Billington with the 6M11 Hunterston–Fiddlers Ferry, seen here on Wednesday 4 September 2013.

No. 56105 passes Taylors House at Clitheroe with the 6J37 Carlisle Yard–Chirk loaded log train, on Tuesday 13 August 2013.

A Network Rail train which is led by DRS 'tractor' 37405, top and tailed with 37419, passes Taylors House at Clitheroe with the 1Q13 Carnforth–Carlisle via Blackpool North and Blackburn, on Tuesday 13 August 2013.

Direct Rail Services 'tractor' 37419, top and tailed with 37405, passes Taylors House at Clitheroe with the 1Q13 Carnforth–Carlisle via Blackburn and Blackpool North test train, on Tuesday 13 August 2013.

Although the service is usually worked by a Class 56, due to problems at Derby 66849 stepped in to work the 6S96 Thursdays-only Sinfin–Grangemouth empty TEA tanks back north as it passes Preston, on Thursday 8 August 2013.

On hire from Freightliner intermodal services, 66569 passes Clitheroe with the 6M11 Hunterston ex Killoch –Fiddlers Ferry loaded coal on Thursday 1 August 2013.

EWS/DBS say goodbye to working the 6K05 before they hand it over to rival company DRS. No. 66087 is seen passing Taylors Bridge at Clitheroe on the second-to-last day of working the 6K05 Carlisle Yard–Crewe Basford Hall departmental train, Friday 19 July 2013.

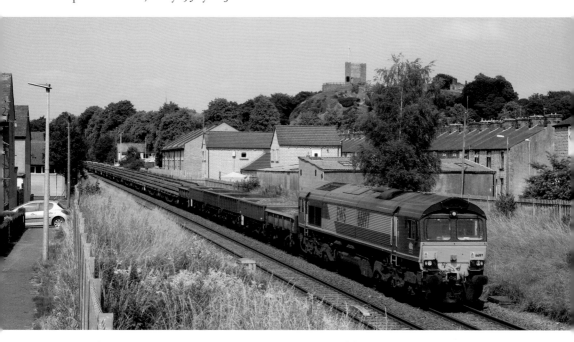

Run by DB Schenker but still in EWS livery, 66197 passes Clitheroe Taylors House with the 6K05 Carlisle Yard–Crewe Basford Hall departmental train. This service will be routed via Bolton and Manchester due to engineering works in the Wigan area and is seen here on Wednesday 17 July 2013.

LMS Jubilee Class 45699 *Galatea* passes Horrocksford Junction at Clitheroe with the 1Z52 Lancaster–Carlisle 'The Fellsman', seen here on Wednesday 17 July 2013. No. 47580 was behind the steam locomotive due to Network Rail's steam ban.

DB Schenker had just won a new contract out of Castle Cement at Clitheroe when 66155 was photographed passing Clitheroe on Tuesday 16 July 2013. This was the second working of the 6Z35 Clitheroe Castle Cement–Avonmouth.

The 6K05, which is now run by DRS, is seen passing Barrow foot crossing near Whalley with 66069 in charge. The train runs from Carlisle Yard to Crewe Basford Hall on weekdays only, and is seen here on Tuesday 16 July 2013.

With Carnforth not being far away, the West Coast Railway Company uses the back lines to work test runs. BR (SR) rebuilt Bulleid Light Pacific 34046 *Braunton* passes Barrow foot crossing near Whalley with the 5Z50 Carnforth–Carnforth test run via Clitheroe and Blackburn, on Tuesday 16 July 2013.

No. 57304 *Pride of Cheshire* manages to escape from the confines of Preston station. It is seen here sat back at Preston, awaiting departure while working the 5Z41 Kilmarnock–Wembley InterCity depot, dragging the Virgin 'Pretendolino' stock which has been contracted to be moved back south by DRS after maintenance at Hunslet-Barclay.

No. 60019, one of many DB Schenker super tugs, passes the first station in the UK to become eco-friendly, Accrington, while in charge of the thrice-weekly 6E32 Preston Dock–Lindsey oil refinery return empties, on Wednesday 10 July 2013.

No. 60019 approaches Blackburn with the 6E32 Preston Dock–Lindsey oil refinery empty tank train, and is seen from the Wainwright Bridge, otherwise known as Ainsworth Bridge, on Wednesday 10 July 2013.

LMS Stanier Class 8F 48151, built for pulling freight, passes under Wainwright Bridge at Blackburn while in charge of the 1Z52 Lancaster–Carlisle 'The Fellsman' on Wednesday 10 July 2013.

DB Schenker Class 66 66155 passes Langho with the first ever working of the 6Z35 Clitheroe Castle Cement–Avonmouth, on Tuesday 9 July 2013. Healey Mills depot's driver Pete was in charge.

After being named *EWS Energy* at Knottingley on Saturday 6 September 2008, 66050 passes Blackburn with the 6K05 Carlisle Yard–Crewe Basford Hall departmental service. It is seen here in the afternoon sun on Tuesday 9 July 2013.

It was a very rare sight when 66076 worked the 6E73 Clitheroe Castle Cement–Doncaster Belmont empty coal, on Saturday 6 July 2013 as it passes Langho.

DRS 'Duff' 47501 passes Clitheroe with the 1Z77 Crewe–Ravenglass 'Northern Belle' charter, which ran via Carlisle, on Saturday 25 May 2013.

GBRf don't often come into Lancashire; however, 66733 was seen passing Clitheroe with the oZ33 Crewe–Carlisle route learner, on Tuesday 14 May 2013. The route learner ran for GBRf after the company won the Fiddlers Ferry–Newbiggin gypsum but was handed back to DB Schenker due to GBRf not having enough locomotives.

DCR 31601 works the 5Z32 Kilmarnock–Old Oak Common refurbished First Great Western high-speed train stock past Brock on Saturday 21 July 2012.

LNER Peppercorn Class A1 60163 *Tornado* is on the return journey of the 1Z77 Carlisle–Crewe 'The Cumbrian Coast Tornado', seen here passing Newsholme in the evening light of Saturday 14 April 2010.

In a lucky spell of sunshine, Colas Rail 'Grid' 56096, with 56105 dead in tow, passes Newsholme with the 6V37 Ribblehead–Chirk Kronospan loaded log train, running a day late on Saturday 13 September 2014.

Rail Blue Charters ran a special tour to Carlisle from Ealing Broadway; here we see 67019 on the return leg of the journey, passing Chatburn, working the 1Z43 Carlisle–Ealing Broadway rail tour on Saturday 30 April 2011. No. 67018 was on the rear.

Class 66 66845, now 66746, working for GBRf, is seen passing Chatburn in charge of the 6J37 Carlisle Yard–Chirk Kronospan loaded log train on Friday 29 April 2011.

No. 70003, a GE power unit, is put through its paces as it screams up the 1 in 80 incline of Whalley Bank with the 6M32 Killoch–Crewe Basford Hall Freightliner Heavy Haul service in late evening sunlight. For added weight on top of the nineteen loaded HXA coal hoppers, 66514 was dead at the rear of the train, hitching a lift back to Crewe. The coal was destined for Rugeley power station.

Built under gaslight in Romania, 56312, ex 56003, passes Bamber Bridge with the 1Z66 Bristol Temple Meads–Carlisle charter service. No. 66148 was hidden behind the Class 56 for company and to provide train heat. It is seen here on Saturday 22 May 2014.

Due to engineering work, the 4S13 Earles Sidings–Carlisle new yard got diverted via Clitheroe. The empty coal is seen passing Rimington with a convoy of DBS Class 66s, 66004, 66109, 66149, 66155 and 66070. This photograph was taken on Saturday 1 May 2010.

Clitheroe cement works held their open day over the weekend of 30 August 2008. A special guest at the open day was 60029, which carried the name *Clitheroe Castle*. Unfortunately, the Class 60 no longer carries the name and has been placed in stores. However, DB Schenker super tug 60024 has been named *Clitheroe Castle* in its memory.

The first ever Class 60 to work the 6S00 Clitheroe–Mossend loaded cement is seen here passing Taylors House at Clitheroe with the then unbranded silver aluminium JPA tanks. The train was diverted via the West Coast Main Line due to engineering work on the Settle & Carlisle, and is seen here on Friday 4 July 2008.

EWS-stickered 92019 *Wagner* passes Brock with the southbound 6O60 Mossend–Dollands Moor empty china clay tanks, on Friday 2 May 2008.

Virgin Trains bodysnatcher 57308 *Tin Tin* drags Pendolino 390042 past Gisburn with the diverted 1M18 Glasgow Central–London Euston. The Class 57 took over the train at Carlisle and would be removed at Preston. It is seen here on Sunday 15 April 2007.

DRS Class 66 66411, the original *Eddie the Engine*, works the 4S43 Daventry–Mossend Tesco express, diverted off the West Coast Main Line via Blackburn and the Settle & Carlisle due to the Greyrigg Pendolino derailment. It is seen here passing Rimington on Friday 3 March 2007.

Now owned by DRS, 37405 is seen here at Clitheroe Castle Cement waiting to depart with the 6E73 Clitheroe Castle Cement–Doncaster Belmont empty coal. It was very rare for a member of this class to work this train, which was photographed on Tuesday 8 August 2006.

Opposite top: No. 66411 passes Horrocksford Junction at Clitheroe with the 4S43 Daventry–Mossend Tesco express, which was diverted off the West Coast Main Line via Blackburn and the Settle & Carlisle due to the Greyrigg Pendolino derailment.

Opposite bottom: Bodysnatcher 57307 passes Taylors House at Clitheroe with the 0C99 Preston–Carlisle route-learning run on behalf of Virgin Trains staff to practise the route in readiness for the diversions. It is seen here on Wednesday 23 July 2014.

Freightliner Class 66 66623 leads the 6Z36 Blackburn–Barrow Hill loaded stone hoppers past Portsmouth on the Copy Pit line on Tuesday 19 June 2012. Behind me is the border with South Yorkshire.

Opposite top: A Network Rail train which is led by DRS 'tractor' 37405, top and tailed with 37419, passes Taylors House at Clitheroe with the 1Q13 Carnforth–Carlisle via Blackpool North and Blackburn. It is seen here on Tuesday 13 August 2013.

Opposite bottom: General Electric 70004 approaches Wilpshire tunnel with the 6M11 Hunterston ex Killoch–Fiddlers Ferry power station loaded coal, seen here on Friday 29 April 2014.

Colas Rails 56105 finally makes Wilpshire, running a day late because of problems with the traction motors at Carlisle. It is seen here hauling the 6J37 Carlisle Yard Colas Rail–Chirk Kronospan loaded log train on Saturday 30 August 2014.

Opposite top: EWS tractor 37174 wakes up the neighbours as it passes through Clitheroe in the early morning sun while working the 6C02 Crewe Basford Hall–Carlisle yard departmental service. This service returns later in the day as the 6K05 and is normally routed via the West Coast Main Line; it is seen here on Wednesday 11 May 2004.

Opposite bottom: DRS 'Duff' 47802, top and tailed with 47501, passes Rimington with the 1Z76 'The Mersey Fellsman', which ran from Crewe to Carlisle via Liverpool Lime Street and the Settle & Carlisle, seen here on Saturday 12 June 2010.

DB Schenker Class 60 60039 powers past Gisburn with an unidentified engineering train working off the Settle & Carlisle to Crewe Basford Hall, photographed on Sunday 11 May 2008.

Opposite top: DRS 'Choppers' 20308 and 20309 work the 1Z20 Stratford-upon-Avon–Carlisle rail tour on behalf of Cheshire Cat Tours, and it is seen here thrashing past Chatburn on Saturday 7 July 2012.

Opposite bottom: Fragonset Class 47 47703 passes Horrocksford Junction at Clitheroe with the 1Z54 'The Edinburgh Fellsman', which ran from Layton near Blackpool to Edinburgh Waverley. The now preserved Brush Class 47 sadly no longer runs on the main line. It was seen here on Saturday 23 September 2006.

A DRS convoy, 66429, 66303, 47828 and 47790, passes Clitheroe train station with the 0K05 Carlisle Kingmoor DRS–Crewe Basford Hall light engine movement, on 19 September 2014.

Opposite top: Virgin-liveried bodysnatcher 57305 is seen passing Gisburn with the diverted 1M18 Glasgow Central–London Euston. The Class 57 was put on at Carlisle and dragged 390013 over the famous 72-mile Settle & Carlisle to Preston, where the Pendolino would carry on its journey to London. It is seen here on Saturday 12 May 2007.

Opposite bottom: Scotrail-liveried 90021 was seen at Preston on Friday 13 November while working the 1P05 Fridays-only London Euston–Preston service. The train then works back to Wembley empty stock.

After a valiant effort working solo due to issues with 20312's multi system, 37603 finally boiled its coolant, resulting in a total loss of power just back from this location. After a few minutes paused, the radiator fan had brought the coolant temperature back down far enough to gain power with a little assistance from 47805 on the tail end. The service was the 1Z87 11.45 Blackpool North–Blackpool North mini rail tour via the Pennines, which attacks the 1 in 68 gradient towards Copy Pit Summit.

Opposite top: DRS tractors 37606 and 37602 were seen working the 6K05 Carlisle Yard–Crewe Basford Hall departmental service on Thursday 6 March 2014, and are photographed here passing Gisburn.

Opposite bottom: DB Schenker-liveried 66114 eases down through the scenic Lancashire hills at Rimington while in charge of the 4M00 Mossend Down Yard–Clitheroe empty VTG cement tanks, on a very dull Monday 12 May 2014.

DBS 66101 passes Gisburn while in charge of the 6Z76 Newbiggin–Warrington Arpley yard on Monday 12 May 2014. In the background stands the old Gisburn signal box, which sadly closed on 18 March 1981 when the absolute section was extended to Horrocksford Junction and Hellifield signal boxes. The signal box is now privately owned.

Opposite top: Freightliner 66610 sits in the old Rimington railway station, which is no longer in use – the former station closed in July 1958. Network Rail was replacing the Down section between Hellifield and Clitheroe in readiness for more freight services. This photograph was taken on Friday 13 June 2008.

Opposite bottom: Running as 0Y10, the Carlisle Yard–Crewe Basford Hall service sees a Freightliner convoy consisting of 70002, 70016, 70010, 66605 and 66529, which is seen here passing Brownhill in the early morning light on Monday 1 April 2013.

DB Schenker Class 66 66105 coasts past Gisburn with the 4M00 Mossend Down Yard–Clitheroe Castle Cement, on Wednesday 5 June 2013. This train runs on Mondays, Wednesdays and Fridays only.

Opposite top: Direct Rail Services' low-emission Class 66 66301 pulls into Preston Up and Down goods loop with the 4S45 Daventry–Mossend container service; this service is no longer DRS-hauled as DB Schenker won the contract. It is seen here on the evening of Wednesday 21 May 2014.

Opposite bottom: Freightliner Class 66 66510 passes Taylors House at Clitheroe with the 6M32 Killoch–Crewe Basford Hall Freightliner Heavy Haul coal service. This train didn't run so often and stopped around a couple of weeks later. It is seen here in the late summer sun as it coasts down towards Whalley on Thursday 24 June 2010.

Seen on the rear of the 0K05 is 'Northern Belle'-liveried 47790 *Galloway Princess*. The Class 47, which is owned by DRS, was getting moved to Crewe in readiness to work the next day's 'Northern Belle'. It is seen here with sister 47828 and DRS sheds' 66429 and 66303 on Friday 19 September 2014. The working was the 0K05 Carlisle Yard–Crewe Basford Hall.

Direct Rail Services bodysnatcher 57307 *Lady Penelope*, normally on Thunderbird duties, is seen approaching Accrington with the return 1Z41 'Northern Belle' special from Oxenholme to Nottingham on Friday 12 September 2014.

In top and tailed mode, we see EWS Class 66s 66158 and 66111 as they pass over Gisburn Viaduct with an unidentified engineering train working off the Settle & Carlisle to Crewe Basford Hall, on Sunday 11 May 2008.

West Coast Railway Company stepped in to help Network Rail clear the lines around Buxton. Here we see 37516 and 47760 passing Taylors House at Clitheroe with the 1Z99 Carlisle New Yard–Buxton Urs snowplough move, photographed on Wednesday 27 March 2013.

Still in EWS livery, 60065 *Spirit of Jaguar* was sounding well with the Mirlees Power unit. The DB Schenker Class 60 still hasn't been put through the super tug scheme and is seen here passing Rishton with the 6E32 Preston Docks–Lindsey oil refinery empty bitumen tanks on Monday 12 May 2014.

Direct Rail Services Class 37 37688 slowly pulls into Morecambe with the 6C52 Heysham nuclear power station–Sellafield nuclear flasks. No. 57007 was on the rear end, ready to work the train back north. This photograph was taken on Tuesday 15 July 2014.

Direct Rail Services driver Ian Tunstall pauses at Clitheroe Castle Cement reception sidings with the inward-bound 1Z20 Crewe–Clitheroe Castle Cement rail tour, seen here on Saturday 31 May 2014. This was as far as the train could go due to Network Rail's boundary in the sidings.

Network Rail's 'Flying Banana' power cars, 43062 and 43013, pass Lancaster with the 1Q26 Glasgow Central–Crewe CS on Tuesday 15 July 2014.

It is rare to see a pair of DRS choppers on the nuclear flasks due to them normally being in the York area for engineering trains and RHTT duties. However, 20312 and 20304 are seen passing Hest Bank with the slightly delayed 6K73 Sellafield–Crewe flask train on Tuesday 1 July 2014.